Motivational B

This Edition Includes:

Boost Your Motivation with Powerful

Mindfulness Techniques & Success

Secrets (NLP)

By James Adler

Copyright ©2016

The scanning, uploading, and distribution of this book via the Internet, or via any other means, without the permission of the author is illegal and punishable by law. Please purchase only authorized electronic editions, and do not participate in or encourage electronic piracy of copyrighted materials.

All information in this book has been carefully researched and checked for factual accuracy. However, the author and publishers make no warranty, expressed or implied, that the information contained herein is appropriate for every individual, situation or purpose, and assume no responsibility for errors or omission. The reader assumes the risk and full responsibility for all actions, and the author will not be held liable for any loss or damage, whether consequential, incidental, and special or otherwise, that may result from the information presented in this publication.

The book is not intended to provide medical advice or to take the place of medical advice and treatment from your personal physician. Readers are advised to consult their own doctors or other qualified mental health professionals regarding the treatment of medical conditions. The author shall not be held liable or responsible for any misunderstanding or misuse of the information contained in this book. The information is not intended to diagnose, treat or cure any disease

Contents

Book 1 Motivation

Boost Your Motivation with Powerful Mindfulness Techniques and Be Unstoppable

By James Adler

Copyright ©2016

Introduction: What is Motivation?

We all have goals in life. You are reading this book because you are looking for inspiration and techniques that will increase your motivation and bring you closer to your goals. Maybe you want to get in shape. Maybe you want to excel in your career. Maybe you want to be an outstanding musician or artist, or pursue some other outlet for your creativity. In general, any time we want something, we are trying to get from where we are right now, to where we would like to be—from *Point A* to *Point B*. And to move along the path between these two points, we need fuel for the journey.

Motivation is the fuel that drives you towards your goals. It comes from desire, and from a vision of your ideal future. It is the emotional energy that pushes you along your journey to actualizing your dreams.

Like any other kind of energy, motivation can be strong or weak, concentrated or scattered. If your motivation is weak or vague, you will not make much progress. You will feel dissatisfied and wonder why you feel so much inner resistance to achieving your goals. You may even have a sense of low physical and psychological energy. It will seem that something is *missing*.

With strong motivation, you will feel energetic, focused, and happy. You'll have a strong sense of direction and purpose, as well as a feeling that you're *moving towards your ideal future* at a pretty good clip. When obstacles get in your way, you will cheerfully find ways to remove them or steer around them. Much of the time, it will even seem as if your path is clearing itself before you, to make way for you on your journey.

It's an obvious choice: if you had to pick strong or weak motivation, wouldn't strong motivation win hands down? I know I always prefer that feeling of energy and purpose that comes with strong motivation over listlessness, boredom, and hesitation.

One of the important things to understand about motivation is the difference between *extrinsic* and *intrinsic* motivation. *Extrinsic motivation* comes from outside you. It could come from pressure at work, or from your family or friends. It could be that somebody planted an idea in your head that you should do this or that. Whatever the case, the problem with extrinsic motivation is that it doesn't come from what you really want. That's why it can't really give you the drive and force that you need to accomplish your goals—and even if you do accomplish them, you won't feel very satisfied for very long, because you didn't *really* want to.

Intrinsic motivation, on the other hand, comes from within you. When you *really want* something, and your passion moves you to achieve it—that's intrinsic motivation. To have this kind of motivation, you need clarity about yourself and your desires and goals, and you need to have the confidence that comes from knowing that you are good enough to have big dreams. That comes from self-knowledge and self-love—and that's where meditation comes in.

Steps for this chapter

- Stop and think about the various things you are trying to do in your life, and ask yourself whether your motivation is intrinsic or extrinsic. I find it helpful to write these things down—something about putting my thoughts into the written word brings the big picture into sharper focus.

- Consider the qualities associated with strong and weak motivation, respectively. Look at your own life and situation and see which qualities are at work. Do you feel inertia, weariness, low mood levels, distraction, or lack of clarity? Or do you have focus, energy, drive, and cheerfulness?

At this point, just *look* at your life and yourself; don't worry about trying to change anything just yet. The willingness to take a look at yourself with an honest and unflinching eye is a powerful and transformative mindfulness practice by itself.

The purpose of this is not to be overly critical and to beat yourself up over your shortcomings. We are not trying to evaluate anything as "good" or "bad;" we are just opening a space for self-honesty and coming into contact with the reality of our situation. In fact, your willingness to build an honest relationship with yourself is a good sign, and a good reason for you to rejoice and feel optimistic!

Free eBook & Newsletter

Your Exclusive Information & Inner Circle Updates

Are you interested in personal development and related topics?

Join *our Holistic Wellness Books Newsletter* & start receiving the most revolutionary P.D tips to help you on your journey.

You will be the first one to find out about our latest releases (eBooks, books, audiobooks and courses) and receive amazing discounts and bonuses!

As a welcome gift, you will receive a **free copy** of our bestselling eBook: *"Affirmations"*:

Simply visit the link below to get it now and join our newsletter (no worries, we don't send spam, only valuable information you will love):

www.bitly.com/affirmationsfree

Chapter 1 Mindfulness for Unlimited Motivation

If you're interested in holistic living, you're probably already familiar with mindfulness. After all, it's all the rage right now, and for good reason. The rise of the mindfulness revolution is fueled by tons of scientific research that shows mindfulness's many benefits, has been widely reported in the media—both traditional and social—and is spearheaded by influential figures like meditation expert Jon Kabat-Zinn and psychologist Daniel Goleman.

But at this point, you might be asking yourself what mindfulness meditation has to do with motivation. After all, doesn't meditation have to do with just resting and being content? And if motivation is anything, it's the drive to achieve or gain something. Won't all that contentment get in the way of the motivation to achieve and change? It seems that meditation and motivation should be opposites.

But meditation is about more than contentment and peace of mind. Meditation is about clarity and living in an honest, straightforward relation to your world. Meditation does not just make a permanent dent on your cushion. It also makes a deep impact on the way you live your life.

Recent decades have seen a groundswell of research into the benefits of mindfulness meditation. Mindfulness's many benefits are now a part of general public knowledge and accepted scientific fact. Among these benefits are:

- deeper concentration and less tendency to distraction
- the ability to focus on the present moment
- an increase in nonjudgmental awareness
- the ability to see your emotions objectively
- letting go of outdated identities
- a general increase in positive emotions

Are you starting to see how this could benefit your

life and your motivation? We will talk about these benefits in more depth later, and then look at some exercises for really taking advantage of them to increase your motivation, but first I want to describe the general practice of mindfulness meditation so that we have a better context for understanding how it has such transformative power for giving you the energy and enthusiasm you need on your road to achieving your goals and dreams.

How to practice mindfulness meditation

Practicing mindfulness meditation is quite simple and does not require a lot of preparation or training. Anyone can get into it. All you have to do is make a little time. *Learning how* to do the practice *is* the practice.

To begin with, set aside five to ten minutes of your day, every day. Find a quiet place to sit. Traditionally, you sit on a cushion or a mat, but you can sit on a chair if you like. You can even lie down. Whatever works for you.

If you are sitting, sit with your back straight. Your eyes can be open or closed; it's up to you. You may find that closing your eyes helps keep you from distraction, at least in the beginning.

The basic practice of sitting meditation is just to place your mind on the breath. *Mindfulness* in this context means being mindful of the breath, just following it as it moves in and out. When thoughts and sensations arise, you notice them and simply return your attention to the breath. It does not really matter what kind of thoughts or feelings come up. They could be boring thoughts about what you need to get from the store, or they could be mean, angry, happy, funny, creative, passionate—whatever.

Whatever comes up, just mentally label it *thinking* and return your attention to the breath. That's the nonjudgmental awareness we talked about earlier—whatever comes up, don't try to decide whether it's good or bad, don't accept or reject it. Just gently say to yourself, *Thinking*, and gently redirect your attention to the breath.

As you follow the breath in and out, you want to pay attention to the sensation of the breath—the feeling of the cool in-breath on your nostrils, and the warmth of the out-breath, the rise and fall of your lungs as you breathe in and out, whether the breath is long or short, shallow or deep, hard or gentle, and so on. In general, when meditating on the breath, you don't try to change the quality of the breath, but just let your lungs breathe however is most natural at any given time, and watch that.

Breathing is an effortless, autonomic function of the body, so we normally don't pay any attention to it. It just goes on in the background, all the time. In the practice of mindfulness, however, we don't take the breath for granted. Instead, we learn to appreciate the breath in its simplicity and variation. We develop a sense of wonder at something so simple and so necessary—taking in lungfuls of healthful, life-giving oxygen, which are delivered to the different organs of our body by the circulation of our blood. If we can learn to love and appreciate the simple fact of being alive, we can love ourselves.

When you begin meditating, it may seem that your discursive thoughts, the so-called "monkey mind," have only increased. Actually, nothing has increased; you just never noticed how active your mind is. Just stick with the practice of remaining mindful of the breath. Slowly, the speed of your thoughts will decrease. You will begin to notice and enjoy the vivid richness of the direct, sensory quality of your experience. This is the beginning of coming in touch with a quality of yourself that is fundamentally awake. It is the discovery of an innate source of goodness deep within your being.

Making friends with yourself

By breathing your awareness to the breath and

learning to appreciate the simplicity of the present moment, you develop a sense of love for yourself that is not based on stories that you tell yourself, your wishes, likes and dislikes, who you tell yourself you want to be, negative thoughts, and so on. Instead, this newfound self-love is based on a direct, honest relationship to your own mind. This relationship is what has been called *making friends with yourself.*

The very act of meditation is an act of kindness to yourself. By setting aside time to rest and watch the breath, you are demonstrating a willingness and a commitment to sit with yourself quietly and gently. That is an act of compassion, a declaration of unconditional friendship to yourself and a willingness to get to know your own mind and heart more deeply.

It may sound strange to hear, but most of us do not really know ourselves that well. That's because we never take the time to get to know ourselves. So it's important to take that time, to slow down and rest. In this state of rest, we become more familiar with our own thoughts and feelings. Through the process of making friends with ourselves in meditation, we equip ourselves with self-love and self-compassion. Thus we can forgive ourselves when we make mistakes, or offer ourselves gentle encouragement and advice when we feel overwhelmed or anxious. This becomes a safeguard against the pessimism that attacks our motivation.

Deeper Concentration

It's easy to see how improving your concentration can increase your motivation to achieve your goals. In our daily lives, we're assailed from all sides by distractions and events vying for our attention. Meditation helps keep us on track by reducing the noise inside our heads. With more mindfulness, we will feel empowered to work towards our goals without going off track.

By bringing us into the present moment, mindfulness meditation helps induce a creative state of awareness psychologists call *flow*. Flow is full absorption in an activity with energetic focus and enjoyment. Research shows that mindfulness increases flow, focus, sharp thinking, self-control, and even the ability to meet deadlines.

Focus on the present moment

In increasing your motivation, it's often helpful to clarify what you want for the future. If you know your desired outcome, that positive vision of the future can give you the energy that spurs you along on your journey to success.

But it's just as easy to fall into the trap of imagining the possibility of failure, disaster, and worst-case scenarios, or succumbing to negative, discouraging memories from the past. When that happens, we feel burdened by negative emotions, our energy and drive diminish, and we lose our motivation.

Instead of causing us to dwell on the past or imagine the future, mindfulness brings our awareness into the present moment. With mindfulness, we cultivate an appreciation for the fullness of our living, breathing situation *right now*. This appreciation for the now lifts our spirits, increases our energy, and brings out a sense of courage within us that allows us to tackle the many challenges of life with cheerfulness and good humor. Living in the present moment, we feel encouraged and motivated in our lives; we sit on solid ground and are not easily knocked off our balance into discouragement and negativity.

Nonjudgmental awareness

For most of us, all sorts of thoughts come into our mind all the time. There is a constant mental chatter going, a running commentary on every aspect of ourselves and our lives.

Oh, Alicia's dress looks nice, I wonder where she

bought it? I wish I looked as good in my clothes.

My boss is not going to be satisfied with my work this month, which will really hurt my chances of getting a raise.

I shouldn't have said that thing at the party last night, I really made a fool of myself.

And so on. We are always making stories and comments in our heads, judging ourselves, people, places, things, events, and so on as *good* or *bad*. When this negative commentary turns inward, we can find ourselves doubting our abilities and undermining our own efforts.

Mindfulness brings us in touch with a *nonjudgmental* awareness, which is not concerned with deciding if things are good or bad, pleasurable or painful, desirable or undesirable. Whatever arises in our mind or outside in the world, we learn to accept it without judgment. In this way, meditation allows us to make friends with ourselves, fundamentally—to be kind and loving to ourselves.

In the context of motivation, nonjudgmental awareness comes to our aid because it keeps us from sinking into discouragement, pessimism, and self-doubt. Because we are making friends with ourselves through the practice of mindfulness, we do not critique and nay-say every aspect of our performance; instead, we learn to feel a natural, gentle encouragement that comes from within. Thus our self-confidence and positive motivation are buoyed by a tide of self-love and inner gentleness.

Emotional objectivity

Connected with the idea of nonjudgmental awareness is emotional objectivity. As human beings, we cannot just mechanically go through our life performing our functions like robots. We're emotional creatures with a rich, colorful inner life full of love and hate, anger, happiness, hope, fear, and so on.

But although emotions are part of the richness of our being, it is all too easy to get swept up in them and lose all sense of perspective. That makes it easy to get knocked off track. Since motivation is an emotional force, it too can get swept away by the current of strong feelings.

Mindfulness meditation allows us to abide in and maintain perspective about our emotions. That does not mean cutting ourselves off from emotional energy, like performing an amputation. What it does mean is increasing our sense of clarity, so that we can look at our emotions honestly, without getting hooked by them or rejecting them altogether.

That is an invaluable resource when we are working towards our goals. The emotional objectivity afforded by mindfulness gives us clarity about what we want and why we want it. It also allows us to keep some distance and perspective when powerful feelings come along that threaten to undo our hard work or blow us off course.

Moving past outmoded identities

One of the things that meditators notice about their minds is that, usually, when we are not being mindful, there is a constant stream of thoughts going on about this or that. These thoughts take the form of statements and judgments about ourselves and the world. Emotions color these thoughts, so that some of them are hopeful and some fearful, some passionate and some aggressive, some jealous, some compassionate and empathetic, some cold and calculating, some generous, and some selfish.

When you take a good look at these thoughts, you'll find that many or most of them use words like *I* or *me*. And a great number of those *I* and *me* thoughts repeat themselves again and again.

The thoughts come at such a rapid pace that they create the illusion of solidity and reality. If you've ever slowed down a film reel you'll know what I'm talking about. At its normal pace, a movie seems to be a continuous flow. If you slow the reel, the illusion is broken, and you see that what seemed like an unbroken continuity is actually made up of many individual frames.

We all have a sense of who we are, where we come from, what we stand for, what we will and will not do, what kind of person we are—a sense of *self-identity*. But this self-identity is much like the illusion created by a film reel. The *I*-thoughts in our mind come so fast that we never have the chance to step back and see the gaps in the picture they create.

Meditation gives us the chance to step back, slow down the film reel of our thoughts, and eye things at a distance. And what we find when we do that is that many of our ideas and thoughts about ourselves are limiting our personal growth and standing between us and our goals by constantly undermining our true desires.

If you find yourself resisting necessary change because "It's just not me," or being overly critical of yourself in a way that thwarts progress, it may be the case that your old identity is becoming an obstacle in your life. In this case, the practice of self-honesty through meditation can help loosen that tight grip on your old, out-of-date identity that is standing in the way of your self-actualization.

Increasing positive emotions

It goes without saying that no one ever gets very far on their path if they are overly negative, self-critical, and feeling down all the time. Even if we do manage to make some good progress, stress and so on leave us in danger of burning out. Negative emotions undermine our motivation and create doubts that stall us on our journey.

Fortunately, mindfulness is proven to increase positive emotions. This has been known for thousands of years, but recent research has corroborated that meditation increases happiness, empathy, emotional regulation, while reducing stress, anxiety, and depression. That's good news for you if you're trying to increase your motivation, because it means that your road to achieving your goals does not have to be a stressful one, and mindfulness will give you the resilience and equanimity you need to handle the emotional bumps in the road.

Bringing mindfulness into everyday life

Mindfulness that stays on the meditation cushion isn't going to bring much overall benefit to you. It might be nice to relax and take a break, but to really experience the power of mindfulness for improving your motivation, you have to take the lessons from your meditation practice and work them into everyday life.

One way to do this is by bringing mindful awareness into simple, everyday tasks. You could start by just being mindful when you're walking. Pay attention to the sensation as your foot touches the ground, the feeling in your legs as they move one after the other, the quality of your breathing as you walk—is it shallow, fast, or short?

You can bring mindfulness into simple activities like washing the dishes or brushing your teeth. Feel the temperature of the water and the slipperiness of the soap as you scrub plates. As you brush your teeth, pay attention to the sensation of the toothbrush as it glides over each individual tooth, the taste and smell of the toothpaste, the foamy later in your mouth.

Whatever activity you are doing, let yourself rest in the awareness of the sensory quality of your experience. Whatever you do is an embodied activity with a physical dimension, and being mindful of that is a very effective way to ground yourself and bring yourself into the present moment.

Once that becomes a habit, it is also incredibly beneficial to practice what's called *mindfulness of mind*. Be aware of what's happening in your mind as you walk, how when you see certain things you get distracted, how different events alter your mood, what kinds of thoughts and emotions come up. Remember, this is a process of getting to know yourself, so you don't have to judge what comes up in your mind—just pay attention to what's going on in there.

Exercise for this chapter

If you've never practiced meditation before, go

ahead and try it out today. Set a time and arrange a quiet place where you will not be disturbed for five or ten minutes. Cross your legs, keep your back straight, and place your mind on the breath as we discussed earlier. Don't spend too long at this— you're just trying to build a familiarity with the practice, not win a mindfulness marathon. Give yourself some time to ease into the practice before you start sitting for longer sessions.

If you already have some experience with mindfulness meditation, that's great! Try to make it a daily practice. I find that morning is the best time for meditating; a morning session sets the right tone for the rest of the day. If you're already maintaining a consistent, daily practice, then all the better. Keep up the good work!

Chapter 2 Mindful Motivation Techniques

So far we've covered the basics of mindfulness meditation, as well as how to work mindfulness into your daily life off the cushion. We've also talked about some of the benefits of mindfulness and how they can help increase your motivation and decrease the obstacles that get in your way.

Now I want to tell you about specific mindfulness techniques to boost motivation. These are meant as supplements to a daily meditation practice. A regular, consistent sitting meditation practice will create the right atmosphere of mindfulness in your life. It sets the mood. Within that atmosphere, we can also use targeted, specific techniques to improve our motivation.

The exercises that follow are meant to help you, but you might find that some are more suitable for you and some are not. Or it may be that some of them work better at some times, and others work better at other times. That's okay. This section is meant to help you start building a tool-kit of techniques that will boost your motivation. Out of this tool-kit, you can pick and choose your favorite tools, whichever ones are right for the job.

Doing in the Now

Consider what's involved in setting goals and working towards them. Dreams, goals, and ambitions come in all shapes and sizes, but let's consider a small one first.

Suppose you're dying to have a banana smoothie. This is a pretty simple and easy goal, and unless you're feeling super lazy, it won't be hard to work up the motivation to achieve it. Chances are, pretty soon you'll be enjoying that smoothie.

Why's that? Well, smoothies are easy to get, of course. They don't cost much and they are available in many places. But another reason you may not have considered is that the goal is not very intimidating. Because it's so easy to achieve, you won't come up against much internal resistance. You won't feel a sense of dread about the hardship, struggle, or boredom you'll have to go through to enjoy that smoothie that rewards your efforts.

Whatever your goal or vision might be, it's probably a much bigger deal than drinking a smoothie, not to mention some way off into the distant future, more or less. That means you're going to have to work hard for it. It also means there will be some irritation, boredom, and difficulty along the way.

That doesn't have to be a problem. In fact, it's a part of life. But when the tasks and work that lie ahead of us seem too big and intimidating, we dread the hard work it will take to complete them. That anxiety leads us to avoid what we need to do. It actually provides a strong *negative* motivation—to procrastinate or dream small.

That's where mindfulness comes in. Instead of trying to accomplish one giant goal, you can try to work on smaller goals instead, one after the other. Break it down so that you're working on just one simple thing at a time, and let yourself get absorbed into that task fully.

Remember how we talked earlier about *flow*? You'll recall that flow is when you get absorbed in what you're doing, and you're enjoying it and feeling energetic at the same time. When you're in flow, you're not dreading or worrying about anything. You're just *doing*.

Break down your goals into smaller pieces, and as you work on each piece, don't think too much about what you're doing—just *do*. Just get into the action of it, become one with it, and let yourself experience what you're doing mindfully.

Let's say your goal is to lose ten kilograms. How will

you do that? Well, you can diet and exercise. Let's focus on exercise. You have to break that down into specific steps, also. So to start with, you could begin running two kilometers every day. And you have to begin with the first day.

On that first run, if you're constantly thinking about how you're going to lose that ten kg, and when will you fit into those old jeans again, etc., you'll start to feel discouraged pretty quickly. Instead of all that over-thinking, you can bring mindfulness on your run with you. Let yourself really feel the sensation of the running shoes slipping onto your feet, the laces tightening. Step outside—is the air warm or hot? Is it dry or muggy? Or maybe the air is cool and crisp with a winter chill, and feels sharp and cold in your lungs.

Then you get going. With each step as you run, your foot hits the ground. You can feel the impact in your legs. As you pick up the pace, you can feel your heart rate going up. As you keep going, your limbs start to tire and your body wants to slow down. Because you're practicing mindfulness as you run, you don't just automatically start walking unconsciously; you are alert and in the moment, absorbed in what you're doing, enjoying it.

As you get absorbed in what you're doing with mindfulness, resting in a nonjudgmental awareness of all sensations and thoughts as they arise, there's no room for dread to come up. You're already doing it, and it's not so bad— in fact, it's kind of nice. It kind of feels good.

Mindfulness of Impermanence

When we have hard work ahead of us and our motivation is low, we sometimes *act* as if we had all the time in the world. So we procrastinate and do something else instead, something that is easy and offers an immediate reward. This may satisfy our desire for instant gratification--at least in the meantime—but in the long term, it will only get us stuck feeling regretful and dissatisfied.

We *know*, if we take a moment to reflect on it, that our time is limited. Mindfulness of impermanence is about taking that moment to reflect. When you find yourself procrastinating, distracted, or feeling to urge to blow off the work you know will bring you closer to your vision of the future, then stop and think to yourself:

Every moment, time is constantly passing me by. Each second ticks away, and seconds become minutes. Minutes become hours, and hours days. Time never stands still, so why act like I can put it on hold?

I won't be the victim of my own inertia. I will be aware of the constant flow of time. Now is the only time to work towards achieving my dreams and goals.

When it's time to start working on your goals, first take a minute to reflect and be mindful of the passage of time. Recall that time is limited. If you don't start doing it now, it will never get done. Get into the habit of renewing your motivation periodically by recalling the mindfulness of impermanence.

Envisioning the future

Everyone will tell you that to motivate yourself, you need to imagine your ideal future. And that's great. The vision of you accomplishing your goals can be an excellent motivator.

What many people won't tell you is that it also provides excellent motivation to imagine what would happen if you just let yourself go. What would your future be like if you gave yourself over to your worst tendencies? What would happen to your life if you let procrastination, inertia, boredom, time wasting, and bad habits take over?

It helps to think about the worst-case scenario because often we are not mindful of the real costs of counterproductive behavioral patterns. These patterns have a way of repeating themselves and turning into habits that are very difficult to change. In order to break them, we first have to understand *why* they are so harmful to us. Then, when they try to assert themselves again, we can summon the will-power to overcome them.

But don't spend too much of your time envisioning a future of doom and gloom. That could cause you to fall into anxiety and depression, which will definite *not* be good motivators. I suggest spending just fifteen to twenty minutes thinking about this worst case scenario one time. It can also help to spend that twenty minutes writing it down in a journal, then closing that journal and putting it away somewhere.

After you have imagined the *bad* future—and I do mean *right after*—you should spend some time envisioning your ideal future. Close your eyes and really build up a rich picture in your imagination. Fill it in with many details— sights, colors, sounds, smells, tastes.

This *your* vision of the future, and it should be strong and compelling.

It is important you don't skip over this second part, because simply imagining a negative future could ruin your mood and your motivation. You need a positive vision to counter the negative one, and then you will have a strong idea of the choices you face and the roads you can go down. You already know which one you want to travel.

If you are struggling with anxiety or depression now, or you have struggled with them in the past, this exercise may not be for you. You might consider passing on it. It's up to you.

It's worth repeating that these exercises should be practiced within the overall context of mental well-being that comes out of a strong mindfulness practice. Then, when negative thoughts and emotions come up, they won't "hook" you so powerfully. Not to mention a regular mindfulness practice is clinically proven to lower stress, depression, and anxiety, which will leave you feeling better and ready to take on life's challenges with gusto.

Eating a healthy diet

In order to keep you functioning at your optimal level, it's important that you eat a healthy, varied diet that gives you the proper nutrition you need.

You may be wondering what this section is doing on a book on mindfulness and motivation. After all, isn't mindfulness about being more aware, appreciating the moment, not getting distracted, and so on? What does all that have to do with healthy eating?

Actually, it has a lot to do with healthy eating. It is now well known that getting the proper nourishment for your body helps you improve and regulate your mood. That shouldn't be a surprise, because the body is the support for the mind. With a shaky and unhealthy support, your mind will also be shaky and unhealthy.

This is not the place to get into the details of planning and keeping a healthy diet. But there are abundant and excellent resources out there that will help you do just that. Remember, you don't have to go so overboard with eating healthy that it becomes your number one concern. In general, it's good to follow the advice *eat to live, don't live to eat. Simply remember to eat a natural, wholesome diet rich in fresh local fruits and vegetables.*

In addition to a healthy diet, you might want to take a few supplements that will improve your mental functioning. One of my favorites is *ashvagandha*, an ayurvedic medicine that research has shown regulates anxiety and stress hormones, increases your energy and mood, and gives you a number of cognitive boosts, such as improved concentration and memory. Do I need to mention that all of those things are important factors in keeping your motivation level high?

Again, you don't need to go overboard and take every supplement known to humanity. Just find one or two that work well for you, to give you an extra push on your journey.

Breaking the chain reaction

Sometimes you're progressing towards your goals, keeping a pretty good pace. You're on a roll, when you suddenly hit a small obstacle. At that time, you might feel an urge to pack it in for the day, go check Facebook, take a walk, or do whatever.

I'm all for taking scheduled breaks. On a regular basis, you need to let yourself rest. Otherwise, you'll just wear yourself down and get burnout. But what happens when, after hitting a rough patch, you decide to take an unscheduled break, and that break is followed by another break, and another? Pretty soon you have an endless series of breaks, and you're left wondering what happened to your time and your motivation.

It's better not to go down that road to begin with. Fortunately, as you mature in your mindfulness practice, you will gain a certain distance from your thoughts, emotions, desires, and urges—a distance we earlier called *emotional objectivity*. The urge to take a detour or procrastinate won't catch you by surprise. You'll actually witness it coming up in your mind—and because you'll be a practiced meditator, you'll just let it be. No need to act on it.

Mindfulness meditation opens up a gap in the usual procedure of our minds. Normally, something happens. We see something, hear something, or think something. That provides the stimulus, which makes us feel one way or another. The many events we come into contact with all the time make us feel good, bad, or neutral. Based on that, we have an urge to act one way or another.

The next step is usually that we form a specific intention to act in a certain way, and then we just carry out the action. But with mindfulness, we can arrest the whole process at the urge. When we find ourselves wanting to act in one way or another, a gap just naturally opens up because of the mindfulness practice we've been doing. Within that gap, we can make a free and deliberate choice: take action, or just let it be. Which is the better choice will depend on the situation. But the point is that it's actually possible to break the usual chain reaction that compels us to certain behaviors and assert our own free will.

Chapter 3 What to Do When Problems Come Up

I'd love to tell you that the journey to actualizing your dreams will be all smooth sailing and blue skies. But we all know that all sorts of problems, big and small, come up in life, and your journey will not always be a breeze. Anything worth doing in life is going run into obstacles and difficulties. So here are a few pointers about how to deal with them in a mindful way.

Mistakes

Everybody makes mistakes. They're an inevitable part of life, and we can learn from them. But sometimes we can be too harsh on ourselves for making mistakes, putting a lot of blame on ourselves and feeling guilty or ashamed. This can kill our energy and motivation: we put all that energy into blaming ourselves, and none is left over for actualizing our goals. Not only that, but we feel lousy and discouraged from our path.

Mindfulness is a big help here. Remember that nonjudgmental awareness I talked about earlier? It comes into play in an important way when we make mistakes. Instead of telling ourselves, *I really messed up, I'm such a jerk/fool/loser*, we can look calmly at the causes and conditions that went into the mistake. *A mistake occurred because of XYZ*. Then, since we know how the mistake happened, we can avoid making it again.

It doesn't matter if the mistake is big or small. It could be something as big as losing a friend over something you did or said, or something as small as not checking anything off your to-do list one day. Whatever the case, don't be too hard on yourself.

It bears repeating: Mindfulness meditation is a process of *making friends with yourself*. Do you jump on your friend's case every time he or she makes a mistake? No? Then there's no need to do it to yourself. Be kind to yourself and forgive yourself for the errors that you make. Then summon up the courage to continue on your path, avoiding the same mistakes in the future.

Disappointment and frustration

Disappointment and frustration are a familiar part of everyone's experience, and they are bound to come up. When they do, they will threaten to overturn your motivation. You may feel like just giving up.

That feeling of despair that makes you want to give up is just another strong emotion that arises in your mind, stays for awhile, then subsides again. Don't identify with the emotion and let it grip you.

Instead, think to yourself, *A feeling has come up*, and just let it be. Watch it, feel its texture, what kinds of thoughts come along with it, where the feeling occurs in the body—because, if you pay attention, you'll find that all emotions occur somewhere in the body. Looking closely at your frustration and disappointment, you'll find that the emotion is not some single overpowering force, but is made up of a number of parts. There's a part of it that consists of thoughts, a part that is a sensation felt in the body, a part that is a feeling-tone energy with a certain force and direction.

Don't try to suppress the feeling, but don't give into it, either. If you pay attention to it, mindfully, something remarkable will happen. The emotion will start to dissolve all by itself, without your having to do anything. It will release its energy, and you will be free to direct that energy to a positive purpose.

Stress

A big part of stress is a physiological response in the body that psychologists call "fight or flight" mode. Stress is basically a response to something that your body and brain experience as a threat. So your heart rate increases, your muscles tense up, your breathing accelerates, blood pressure goes up, your digestive system is inhibited.

None of this is a problem if you're staring down a predator in the jungle. In fact, it's a good thing, because it gets you ready to either fight for your life, or run away very fast. And, in the wilderness, you'll need to do one of those things if you hope to live.

But in our hectic modern lives, it's often the case that what our brain experiences as a threat does not go away. So we stay in fight-or-flight for days, months, years. We can't sleep properly, often we don't feel like eating, and we're generally just miserable. Eventually it takes a big toll on our health and can lead to a number of diseases.

The good news is that meditation just by itself is shown to reduce stress very effectively. In addition to that, however, there are a few things you can do to bring your stress levels down. The most important thing to do is find ways to rest. Even if you are very busy, take some *me* time to just relax.

By "resting" I don't just mean sleeping, although that's important, too. I mean doing things that you find intrinsically enjoyable—that you don't have to force yourself to do, because you *want* to do them. That can be enjoying a tasty meal, talking a long walk in the afternoon, going for a swim, spending time with loved ones. Exercise is an excellent method for lowering stress, as is relaxing with friends and family.

The basic idea is that, since your brain thinks you

are in danger, you need to do things that make the brain feel safe. You don't have to force your stress levels down. Just engage in some restful, enjoyable activity, and the stress will go down all by itself.

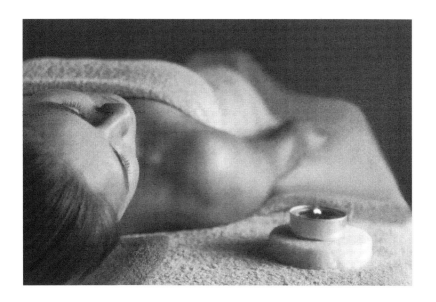

Doubt and fear

Maybe you have all kinds of doubts about yourself, such as thoughts that you're not good enough, or smart, capable, or knowledgeable enough to achieve success. Or maybe you are fearful for the future, imagining all kinds of things that can go wrong.

Remember how we talked about *I*-thoughts and letting go of old identities? The self-doubts that come into your head again and again are an excellent example of *I*-thoughts that are holding you back from your goals. Look at these thoughts directly, but don't engage them with more thinking. Just watch them when they come up. Think to yourself, *A doubt is occurring.* Just label it *Thinking* and let it go.

Fear of things going wrong comes with imagining all kinds of bad scenarios. Yes, I know I told you to imagine a worst-case scenario earlier. That was just a one-time exercise for the purpose of clarifying your motivation. You definitely don't want to make a habit of it.

When you find your imagination wandering to the future and imagining scary scenarios, you know your mind has wandered from the present moment. In that case, gently guide your attention back to whatever you are doing. Don't feel guilty about losing your mindfulness, and don't judge yourself for your wandering mind. Just, again, label the fear *Thinking* and return to the task at hand.

In time you'll find that, whatever you are doing, you are more and more able to "keep your seat." That is, when strong feelings or unexpected events occur, they don't knock you off your balance, but you maintain your equilibrium and deal with things skillfully. But this takes time and practice. Until that day comes, don't get disheartened when you lose your seat; you can always catch yourself and find it again.

Working with low energy

It happens to the best of us. We run out of steam, or we never pick up any steam to begin with. Our mood can best be described as "blah," totally apathetic or maybe depressed. We just don't have any energy to be bothered with anything. Every task we need to do seems like such a demanding and awful chore.

It's not just a matter of this low-energy state sucking all the life out of your motivation. When your energy is low, you have very little confidence in yourself, and other people can sense it. They may avoid you, or ignore what you say, not take you seriously, and so on. Unconsciously, they may even blame you for mistakes that were not even your fault.

Even in meditation, you might slip into a state in which your energy is low and you are not particularly attentive or alert. It may feel like a fog has settled over you. You feel dull and sleepy. In that case, you can imagine that you are sitting on the peak of a mountain, with the bright harsh sun shining above you and the cold wind blowing against your skin. When you breathe in, imagine that a golden light fills your body. This method will restore alertness and energy to your mind when you're sitting.

Off the cushion, plenty of exercise and a healthy diet are important for keeping your energy levels up, as I mentioned above. Get up, go outside, try something new and exciting. If you can manage it, take a vacation and go on an adventure. Whatever you do, don't just sit around and stew in your own juices.

In some cases, however, a lack of energy is telling you something important. It may be that what you are trying to do, what you are trying to accomplish, is not something that you are truly passionate about. In that case, it's a case of intrinsic versus extrinsic motivation. You have no intrinsic motivation to accomplish your goals because, well, the goals didn't really come from *you*.

In such cases, there's nothing for it but to change your life so that you're pursuing what you really value and are passionate about. This requires a lot of self-honesty and courage, but you will find all the inner resources you need through the practice of meditation. A strong mindfulness practice will give you clarity about what you really want and what you really value, as opposed to what you've been *told* you *should* want or value. It will act as a compass guiding you through life and telling you when you're not where you should be—and also, when you're moving in the right direction.

Conclusion

We have covered the basics of what motivation is, as well as the definition of mindfulness and how to practice it. We've discussed the many benefits of mindfulness and how they can help you increase your motivation, as well as how to bring mindfulness off the cushion into your daily life. We've looked at a few techniques that will help you jump-start your motivation when it's down. Finally, we've talked about how to work with a number of problems that can arise and reduce your motivation if you let them—and how to not let them.

You now have all the basic knowledge and tools you need to start practicing mindfulness to increase your motivation *today*. I hope this book itself has given you some inspiration and motivation to begin. I wish you many blessings and all the best on your journey. Good luck!

I wish you success, focus and unlimited motivation,

Until next time,

James Adler

PS. Can I ask you a quick favor? If you enjoyed this book, please take the time to share your thoughts and post a review.

It would be greatly appreciated!

Your review is a great way to let others know of the benefits you've got from mindfulness based motivational strategies. This will not only help others reach their goals, but it is incredibly rewarding for me to know how much my work has benefited others! This way you can help empower others in the way Mindfulness has empowered you...

Book 2 Success Secrets

Change Your Life with Neuro-Linguistic Programming.

NLP Techniques for Personal and Professional Success and Lifestyle Transformation

By James Adler

Copyright © James Adler, 2013, 2015

Introduction

Dear Reader, thank you for taking an interest in my work. It really means a lot to me!

My name is James. I am almost 40 years old (I am feeling much younger though!), and I am really passionate about personal development and motivation. I DON'T believe that things just happen. You can make things happen. Success, motivation, fulfillment, and vibrant health are waiting for you, but you must be willing to learn more about yourself and your abilities. You must take action. This is easier said than done, I know. I used to have this belief also, until I realized how limiting it was.

NLP made me realize that I have the power to unlock my potential. I want to share this experience with you. I want to make it as easy as possible. This book is designed to be a <u>short</u>, <u>practical guide</u> <u>inspired by NLP</u>. My aim is to help you brainstorm to spot your limiting beliefs that stop you from achieving success. Then you will reprogram yourself utilizing some of the strategies discussed in this book.

I do believe that we have lots in common. You might be asking yourself, "Why? I have never even met you, James." It's simple. We both want to design and create lives of our dreams.

We are both committed to learning and getting new skills. Finally, and the most importantly, we are both seekers. You are seeking answers and solutions. You are seeking a better quality of life where you will do the best you can and be successful. This is why you took interest in this book.

We are both seekers.

I have found successes through NLP and I know you can too. I want to share my experience and inspire other people to change their lives too.

Use this book as a guide in observing how you feel as a result of what and how you talk to yourself. Observe how such self-talk colors your experiences, puts a limit to what you can accomplish, and limits what is actually possible. I can help you explore and apply NLP for your lifestyle transformation and successful attainment of your goals in life.

You will also realize that some of your past failures were due to your limiting beliefs that were ingrained in you by society and your friends and family members. Not that they did not want you to succeed. They were trying to protect you from the unknown, or they did not know what you are just about to learn.

Finally, you will learn to perceive your past failures as your assets. Often times our past failures make us fearful and as a result we never take the action we should. We associate too much pain with the process of achieving success. With NLP you can change this outdated concept. I believe that one can learn from past failures and even use them as motivators. Each failure makes you stronger and more prepared to face the struggle that is necessary to build success with your own hands. Failure allows you to develop your emotional muscles.

It can be challenging, but we all need to toughen up. NLP will be extremely useful to help you toughen up holistically. All systems must be involved - body, mind, and spirit.

With NLP, you will change your life to become the successful person that you have always wanted to be. You will be given tips on how to set goals and achieve them, and how to use the power of your mind to radiate health to your body to feel youthful vitality. You will also be introduced to the magic of matching and mirroring to forge great relationships. Imagine how you can hold the world in your hands when you touch the lives of the people who matter the most in your life in a positive way! Inspiring others is extremely motivating.

Some people may reject NLP thinking that it has to do with "laws of attraction." Guess what? These two work closely together. There is only one thing that I want you to be aware of. Many people who believe in the law of attraction don't take action. I personally don't like this strategy. Waiting for the unexpected to happen is not effective. I feel that people believe in the laws of attraction because they truly want to change their life. They may be visualizing, feeling, and waiting, but deep inside, they still have this limiting belief that they don't deserve it. The work they have done was not holistic enough. They still need to embark on the journey of self-development.

In my opinion, the key to success is to combine both the law of attraction rules and NLP. The laws of attraction strategies form part of NLP, but NLP goes much deeper inside you. It addresses your old limiting beliefs and the way you interact with yourself and others. If you do it right, NLP can help you change your perception of the world to become more positive and less fearful. We all need this, right? Pessimism and fear often hold us back from taking action. You have probably been there yourself. I have, but I don't want to go back there!

I am now committed to constructing my own reality utilizing NLP tools and strategies.

Finally, the secrets of attracting money will be uncovered

before your very eyes. Again, we are not talking about sitting on a couch and just imagining you are attracting wealth. We want to go deep inside and learn more about ourselves. Why do we perceive money in a certain way? How does it reverberate on our financial reality?

This is going to be an exciting journey, my friend!

With the tools and strategies of NLP, you will have everything you need to be happy and successful: resources, skills, people, and your health. What more can you ask for? So, waste not a single moment and read on. You will realize the power of your thoughts by making everything fall into place to pave the way for a successful new you!

With so much being said about NLP for relationships, I often get asked if NLP is an honest tool. Many people fear that NLP is an evil strategy that manipulates people into doing what we want and when we want. This is untrue. The real NLP is honest and does not promote any form of manipulation or convincing others into following something that is not good for them. I am against all kinds of dishonest practices. Unfortunately, many marketers and salesmen apply those strategies for their own benefit. This is just reality. By learning more about yourself, your subconscious and NLP, you will be able to make yourself stronger. In fact, I would recommend a solid NLP course for all those who are shopaholics or find themselves victim of aggressive advertisement. Of course, practicing the skills you will learn requires time and perseverance. It can't be mastered in a day. It needs to become part of your lifestyle like it is part of mine.

Whenever I go out shopping with family or friends, I notice how prone they are to all those "bargains", "must haves" and "today only" offers. They often get back home with credit card debts, feeling sorry for themselves and not really knowing how this could happen if they were not in need of any of the items purchased. They acted impulsively and now have buyer's remorse.

It all comes down to how someone or something managed to get to your subconscious. NLP can help you become more aware of those patterns.

Back to relationships and NLP

I believe that NLP helps you develop empathy towards others and their way of thinking. Understanding what others think, why they think that way and the factors that provoked their thinking is crucial if you want to establish any form of deep discourse with them.

Let me give you a simple example. Let's say that you are in your 20s and you want to move abroad to learn about another culture and a new language. Your parents tell you to stay where you are and look for a job. You disagree with them and say they are not right and that the way they live is boring. This leads to further arguments.

Here's the truth. Nobody is right or wrong. You are both right in a way. The important thing to realize is that you are thinking and acting from different perspectives. You are young and you grew up in a globalized world where the internet makes it really easy to travel, plan, and still communicate with your family. Your parents may not be used to this modern, global lifestyle. When they were young, very few people they knew would move to another country. It used to be more difficult. In this day and age, traveling is not only a "2 weeks' vacation" concept. Many people work online for their company or running their own businesses. They can be mobile. Moreover, English is a global language and so more and more people want to learn it, hence there are plenty of English-teaching jobs available world-wide, and many young people use it to their advantage and become international teachers in exotic countries.

So, if you are that 20 year old kid, instead of arguing with your parents, you should perceive the world through their eyes and realize that all they want to do is to protect you. Be grateful for that. There are many people in this world who have never even met their parents. It is a normal thing that parents do grumble a bit, right?

Once you have shifted your perception and developed more empathy it will be a better time to sit down and talk to your parents again. Thank them for being worried about you and explain to them all the possibilities waiting for you abroad. Tell them how you can keep in touch and how this process can even strengthen your relationship. You should have evidence prepared to show them, such as how you can make travel plans, how you will communicate, and what your plans are to provide yourself with income to live. Give them examples of how this experience will benefit you personally.

In my experience if you move to another city, state or even country, you may start getting on better with some of your family and friends. Distance really can make the heart grow fonder.

I hope that this simple example helped you understand the infinity of solutions that NLP provides in the real world. There is no reason to be an expert in the NLP field to actually apply it in order to improve your quality of life on all levels.

I don't claim to be a NLP guru. I want to be your friend who accompanies you in your journey (sharing his own experiences that can be helpful). Perhaps you will relate better to real stories instead of just some definitions and school books. I have no intention of becoming a life coach. I don't want to tell you that a certain lifestyle is the best one and that you must follow through with what I say or do. I am not a big fan of step by step programs, or "proven steps and strategies." My intention is to help you brainstorm so that you can realize many new things about yourself and how they either stop you from being successful or make you successful.

It's all inside you! It's up to you to decide what to do with it. There are many "lifestyle templates" you can use. However, in my opinion, the best you can do is to screw all of them and create your own way.

Thanks again for purchasing this book. I hope you enjoy it!

To your success,
James

Chapter 1: What is NLP?

NLP is a popular acronym which represents the three elements of an innovative approach to communication, self-improvement, and mind conditioning. It is meant to have the effect of planned positive change in various aspects of a person's life. The approach capitalizes on the posited interconnection among the following processes:

- Neurological processes (thus, **Neuro**) of one's brain and the nervous system;
- **Linguistic** or the process of communicating with one's self, as well as with others; and
- **Programming** or the patterns of behavior one learns or adopts based on experiences and occurrences in daily life.

Hence, NLP is for anyone who wants to make a change in their lives towards personal and/or professional development and success. NLP has been around for about four decades now and was initially tapped as an adjunct to psychotherapy. However, its early success in therapeutics spread to other fields, particularly in education and business. Additionally, NLP is applied in sports, consultancy and coaching, training, recruitment, sales, and in practically all facets of life where one wants to attain transformation for the better to achieve success.

From the original aspirations of its creators, linguistics professor John Grinder and psychology student Richard Bandlcr, NLP is meant to model or emulate outstanding therapists in order to generate similar results. Experts who supported the approach developed NLP for modeling and replicating behavior or skills that lead to successful outcomes. Grounded on a unique methodology targeted on specifically identified outcomes, NLP endeavors to address things or issues that affect how people perceive and do things, but which they are not aware of. **In other words, NLP is about bringing the unconscious to awareness.**

To illustrate, when you tell yourself that you do not have enough skills to turn your brilliant idea into a winning business proposal to a prospect investor, such a message to yourself stimulates unconscious thoughts, pictures, and feelings about proposal writing that leads you to formulate and present the proposal in a less than helpful way. You know you have the skills, but your self-doubt hinders your confidence and you won't meet your full potential.

How NLP Can Help You

NLP guides you to observe how you feel as a result of what and how you talk to yourself, and how such self talk colors your experiences, puts a limit to what you can accomplish, and to what is actually possible. Without the need to bore you with the hard facts and technicalities of NLP, this book takes you on a guided tour to applying NLP for your lifestyle transformation and success for your goals in life. Remember, how you feel as a consequence of the language you convey to your own self colors your feelings about how you see the world. Through such self-talk, you paint your day bright or grey.

As you turn the pages, pay close attention to the secret that is revealed about the following:

- How you block yourself from being as successful as you want to be
- How you do not take action about the change you intend to make
- How you are not able to think up solutions or alternative courses of action for your goals

Who Can Benefit from NLP

NLP is for people that admire other people who excel at what they do, and for people who would like to write their own success story as well. If you have set goals, but find success at such goals elusive, read on. If you want to get rid of negative emotions, read and practice this unique approach for success.

In a nutshell, NLP will light your path towards success by:

- Organizing your thoughts - the neuro aspect
- Positively representing the mental imagery of how you want to view the world and communicating it - the linguistic aspect
- Modeling and reinforcing the behavior that will trigger memories and responses to the condition that has to be changed or resolved based on desired outcomes - the programming aspect

There is also another extremely important element of NLP that many coaches and motivational speakers (Tony Robbins, for example) utilize and it comes down to working with your physiology. This is really simple. Recall a certain event from your past when you were and felt successful or when something extremely positive happened. I will share some of my own experiences to help you brainstorm.

1. Back in high school, the girl I had a crash on agreed to go out with me!

I can still remember feeling this "buzz." I was ecstatic when she said yes! I felt like a winner. The feeling of "everything is possible" dominated me.

EXCERCISE- I close my eyes and I recall the feelings. As a result, my physiology changes. By the way, did you know that even the color of your eyes may slightly change when you are feeling extremely happy?

I walk as a winner. My head is kept high. My body emanates self-confidence.

Now compare this to getting rejected (Yes, I also got rejected dozens of times). I would look and feel sad. I would keep my head down and I would feel like a loser.

The key is being able to recall the positive situation. Whenever I face a situation where I might be potentially rejected (a job interview, asking someone out, proposing a project to my boss, etc...) or whenever I plan my goals, I use my physiology to put myself in this amazing emotional state of success.

If you do get rejected, it won't feel like the end of the world for you because you will begin to believe in yourself. Your perception of success and failure will be changed. You will accept failure as a part of success.

Now, think about your voice. How do you sound when you are happy? How do you sound when you are disappointed? How do you sound when you are excited? Of course, it's not only about how you talk. There is also the way you walk, stand, sit, breathe and think. We very often take it for granted and never analyze it.

I suggest you take a few deep breaths and reflect on your day today. What happened today and how did you feel? What were you thinking? What could have gone differently?

This is the first step to becoming more aware of your body, mind, emotions, and what is happens contrary to your will. Guess what? You have the power to control it.

This is something that many holistic therapists and healers (for example Reiki therapists and other energy healers) utilize. They very often tell you to focus on only one feeling or emotion at a time, or, just like the Reiki precept says, focus "just for today". It is important to learn how to focus on just one thing and reject the concept of multitasking that often kills our awareness and ability to inspire the body and mind connection.

Now this is very important and I suggest you take a note of it. This is a simple exercise that I want you to try next time you feel sad, frustrated, unmotivated, tired, or disillusioned (whatever sorry plight you might be in). Maybe this is how you are feeling now?

1. Realize how you feel. Describe it in your own words. You can write it down or record it on your mobile. Recording is an awesome chance to listen to how your voice sounds in this state.

2. Think what caused this feeling. Get to the root of it.

3. Accept it. Be grateful that this has happened as it made you stronger and emotionally fit.

4. Now, try to look at yourself from the outside. What is your posture? Your facial expression? Do you smile? How do you sound? How do you walk? Write it down and record it.

5. Finally, it's time to shift your feelings and emotions. Think of a situation when you felt like a winner. You can also create it in your imagination. What I like to do is to play some optimistic, energetic songs. My body and mind feel it immediately. I set myself up for a win.

6. Now, keep the positive feelings. You are a winner and achiever. Talk to yourself. Yes, this is absolutely normal! I talk to myself all the time. Use your voice. Make it confident and determined. Slow down your breath and relax. Go through all the positive emotions and feel them once again. Remember that it's not enough to say, "I am happy and I am happy and I am happy," or whatever else you might say. You need to feel it with all of your body, mind and emotions.

7. Now you are an NLP warrior! Congratulations! Doesn't that feel great? The most important and difficult part is now behind you. You can transform negative into positive. For those that believe in the "Law of Attraction" feeling good is also an important step in manifesting success. Good feelings attract good things, events and people. The important part is to practice as much as possible and create your own NLP rituals. The more you do, the more you can control your feelings and emotions. This is not just about repeating some mantras in a meaningless manner. This is about growing and exploring your human potential.

Chapter 2: Use NLP to Achieve Your Goals

NLP does not just pave the way for the achievement of your goal. The approach also guides you towards effective goal-setting. Organizing your thoughts facilitates the design of well-formulated goals that should start with a crystal clear view of WHAT you want, WHY you want it and HOW you talk and think about it. Clearly articulate to yourself what you want by using positive language. To illustrate, you don't say, "I <u>ought to</u> lose this ugly flab of fat as soon as possible." Instead, you say, "I <u>choose</u> to burn three to five pounds a week within the next two months."

You can also start by using these phrases:

- "I will easily…"

- "…because I deserve to…"

- "My goal is to inspire others through my mindful lifestyle"

Forget about using these:
- "we will see what happens…"

- "...maybe when..."

- "...if I manage..." (It's better to say, "When I have successfully completed...")

- "I am not too sure, but I will try..."

- "I probably can't make it but..."

- "I can never lose weight so it's pointless to waste my time." (another limiting belief)

- "A healthy lifestyle and dieting are sacrifices that are really difficult." (limiting belief again)

Prologue to Goal Setting via NLP

Phrasing is an important feature of goal definition in NLP because you want to shift the focus from what you <u>do not</u> want (i.e. - ugly flab of fat) to what you <u>do</u> want (i.e. - burn extra calories). As you say, "ugly flab of fat," you imagine the picture of an obese person, but when you say "burn extra calories," you tend to imagine a leaner body sweating profusely as you work out on a treadmill or sway to the catchy tune of a Zumba routine.

You also harness the power of the word when you use "choose" instead of "ought". The words "need", "ought", and "should" are limiting language, whereas "select", "choose" or "want" are helping or reinforcing language. "As soon as possible" is vague, but "within the next two months" at the rate of "three to five pounds a week" is very clear and more definitive.

When you use "should", or "must" or even "have to" you give your goals some negative meanings; you simply manifest that you just do it because it is your responsibility or someone else tells you to do it. Remember, my friend, you are the number one star here as it's all about YOU and YOUR LIFE. What you choose to say is precious so just stick to what you want and WHY you want it.

Remember, in addition to being very clear about what you want, and use of positive and reinforcing language, goal formulation should follow the SMART criteria:

- Specific
- Measurable
- Attainable
- Relevant
- Time-bound

These are the basics of goal setting. Many people fail to achieve their goals because they never actually took those 5 minutes to formulate them properly.

I spent all my twenties "wanting" to lose weight. My mistake was that I kept saying, "I want to lose some weight" and that was it. I would feel frustrated. Only when I specified exactly how much weight I wanted to lose, when I would lose it, and why I wanted to lose it(I listed dozens of reasons why I finally deserved to lose weight and transform my body into my biggest asset) did I start to change. I planned HOW I was going to achieve it (I chose a diet that worked for me, picked up a personal trainer and got determined to learn everything I could about my body and the process of losing weight.). I managed to be successful, the way I WANTED. I changed my body and my mindset.

My determination and focus were natural and came from my inner self and my own wishes. I also realized why I subconsciously did not want to lose weight. It was my old coach, Mr. Aaron, who made me realize this.

Many of my family and friends also struggled with obesity. Back then, I subconsciously cultivated this limiting belief that, "If I lose weight and become successful, I will no longer fit into my family and their standards." It was my fear of rejection. I would mistakenly believe that I could not participate in family reunions or go out with friends as they would not accept my new, healthy lifestyle. I also feared that my new, healthy, and sexy body would make them feel bad about themselves. This is what was holding me back for over 20 years.

This is how I managed to change my mindset and my perception: I associated pleasure to achieving my goals because I realized that I would actually inspire my family. I knew that I had to learn more about the dietary lifestyle I chose for myself (I chose the Paleo Diet and added lots of greens inspired by the Alkaline Diet. I encourage you to explore the many diet plans out there and choose one that works for you in your lifestyle.). So I would imagine getting new skills such as cooking healthy and delicious food for my family and helping them achieve their weight loss and fitness goals. I would feel all the positive emotions that my family and friends would feel. I even wrote a letter to myself saying "thank you" for all the inspiration.

Thanks to my changed mindset, I felt inspired and guided by my own choices.

I achieved my wellness and weight loss success. I learned so much during this process that I was able to become a "weight loss coach" for many of my family and friends.

This is a very important part of achieving your goals. Think of all the extra benefits and the way you can make a difference to change other peoples' lives. It works! NLP will naturally change your mindset and help you get rid of limiting beliefs, negative self-talk and thoughts that cause inner conflict.

NLP Strategies to Achieve Your Goal

Every goal, big or small, deserves your full time and attention. You should take the time to run through the six simple steps of NLP to optimize success or to affect a change that will lead to success. NLP considers the following strategies in designing goals with the best chance for success;

- Ascertain if what you want to aim for is totally within your control

This step is important because it verifies if your goal is realistic or if you are able to hit your target without depending on someone else's action. If you are an aspiring boxer and aim to turn professional within the next three years, a goal to be a highly-ranked world class fighter is possible. Nevertheless, a goal to compete against Manny Pacquiao in a title match within the next five years depends on whether Pacquiao will remain active in the boxing scene and if he will still holding a championship belt. It's all about taking small steps and creating a bigger picture as a result. Don't try to do too much to begin with, you may end up feeling frustrated and your self-confidence will suffer.

- Endeavor to come up with an indicator that the goal has been attained

This step tackles your measure of success. Without this step, you might end up in a wild goose chase not knowing when to say, "I did it!" To illustrate, a goal of being a successful writer is possible, but what is your own measure of success? For one person, success as a writer may simply be publishing a blog online with a following of 500 readers. Yet for another, being a successful writer means his novel is being adapted as a top-grossing Hollywood film. In NLP, a goal is not complete without a signal of achievement. You need to have your own definition of success and stick to it.

- Zoom out and assess the overall implication of this goal on your life at the present time

Each goal you set makes an impact not only on you, but may also influence others around you. Look at how the achievement of this goal will fit into the bigger picture. If your goal is to own the biggest and most successful local grocery shop, does this success mean you want to see your three competitors close shop? Will you still have quality time for your family? Do you have enough resources to put in more capital without having your eldest quit college?

It's OK to redefine your goals. We all change. Nothing remains the same. There is no point in sticking to the same old goal, just because you want to complete it. If there is no deeper meaning behind it, what's the point? The goal may not be serving our overall idea of success anymore. A good friend of mine had a dream of setting up a massage studio. She tried everything she could, but she realized that the external factors were speaking for themselves – there was no big demand in her area (she did not want to move), there were expensive maintenance costs and taxes in her country and, on top of that, people were not spending extra money due to the national recession and unemployment. However, she went deep inside and analyzed her long-term goals. (She is so inspiring. I find that when I surround myself with inspiring people, I also become inspired! You should find friends that inspire and support you.)

She realized that what drove her to start her own massage studio was not the massage work (even though she loves it), but her passion for helping other people create healthy and balanced lifestyles. She is really into wellness and has a good background in holistic therapies and nutrition. She is also a holistic "from the heart" coach. I think she was born with this ability to inspire and motivate others as she is creative and intuitive, and of course, she has the right NLP mindset.

She also realized that she spent so many years living in Spain and, as much as she enjoyed it, she got a bit tired of sticking to the same culture. My friend, Maria, has a truly international spirit.

Here is what she did: she went through her goals again. She realized that her dream to start a massage studio was not a goal in itself but a means to her main goal which was to make a difference and help others. This is why she decided to change her TOOL.

She struggled financially while sticking only to her idea of local massage treatments. She saw it as a sign to change her tools and strategies; she did not see it as failing. She decided to focus on something else which was...writing!

Even though very few people understood her decision, she decided to turn from the local market and go global. She knew she could contribute to the world and so she changed her tools. She started a blog (wellness and personal development niche) and shared all her wonderful tips. She also rediscovered her old passion of creative writing. She is now a nonfiction author dedicated to wellness, personal and spiritual development, motivation, and many other amazing topics. Most of her books hit the bestsellers lists in the US and other countries.

She told me she felt so utterly grateful for the opportunity of self-publishing, as she could make many new friends, connect to her readers and meet other authors. She can now admit that she does what she loves; her passion is her work. She feels productive and she calls her writing her "global wellness consultation."

In addition, she told me that she felt really blessed thanks to the process of starting an online business. She learned many things about herself, acquired a myriad of knew skills, and eliminated many limiting beliefs (she used to think that the only way to have a business is to do it locally, with local clients). She toughened up, and discovered an entrepreneur spirit inside her. She also realized that Spain was limiting her in many ways and is now planning to move to another country. Thanks to the online work she does, she can be mobile and get back to what she was really committed to in her early twenties - traveling.

She is one of the few people I know who can turn negative into positive. She does it intuitively. She told me she did not know too much about NLP until she met me.

NLP is a mindset and practicing this mindset constantly is how you will find success. I know many certified coaches who know almost everything there is to know about NLP, yet they never use their knowledge to manifest success, or to create a purposeful and meaningful lifestyle. I truly feel in order to manifest success, you not only have to have knowledge of the subject, but you must PRACTICE it. Turn your thoughts into beliefs and actions.

As for continuing her passions, my friend became a volunteer massage therapist because she wanted to contribute to her local community. One of her projects is also to become a travelling massage therapist. She wants to travel, learn new techniques and teach what she already knows to another people. She has defined goals and a nice plan!

Now imagine what could have happened if she had not re-defined her goals and tools?

As she did not have enough money to invest in a local business, she would have gone bankrupt after a couple of months. She would have felt frustrated and would have probably ended up getting a job she hated, something that she wanted to avoid

Based on the macro-perspective of your success in one goal, undertake the next steps. Take note that your other goals may be affected by the success of this one goal. Zoom out on the bigger image to see your life on a wide angle lens. This way, you can program yourself for success.

Life is all about making decisions and adjusting your goals to your current lifestyle. Some people just blindly follow thorough even if the internal or external factors are sending signals that there might be something different and much better waiting for them.

- Envision your goal happening

Create a mental image of this goal as it progresses to fruition. Take yourself down the road as success unfolds right before you in your mind. Close your eyes and see it happen, smell the scent of success, feel its triumph, and experience your life transform as you intend it to be. As you go back to the real world, you actually see your days brighter because you feel so good about success. I suggest you create a vision board and use this step as a part of your morning ritual. Have a cup of tea, coffee, smoothie, or whatever you want to sip on to wake up, and spend a few minutes reviewing your goals. This is so much better than just browsing through the news which is often negative and makes you feel fearful and insecure.

- Conceptualize the plan

As you develop your plan, see yourself not merely writing it or wishing it, but working to get it done. Experience the joy and pride of hitting that goal. Rewind to the past and then fast forward to the future to visualize how success has transformed you. For example, you started as a door-to-door salesman and now you are in charge of several large accounts. You can always go higher and higher. If you are writer, like me, develop a plan of writing more and more books. Whatever product or service you are creating, think big. Don't stop. Read motivational stories of those who made something out of nothing. I love all rags to riches stories of those who changed the world. Use the positivity to inspire you.

Then take an imaginary and leisurely walk down memory lane to retrace the support you received and remember how you motivated yourself. Observe the resources you used and the skills and abilities you marshaled to attain your goal.

Now, focus on the present time. Through such guided imagery, enrich your arsenal of motivation to fully appreciate what it will take to move from this very moment until goal completion. You are programming yourself to hit that goal.

• Perform a dry run

The great thing about NLP is you get to conduct a success drill. This is similar to how organizations practice fire and earthquake drills to give their staff an idea of what might be expected when the real thing happens. The only difference is you perform the dry run in your mind. As you undertake the dry run for success, remember to assume the role you need to. You should make that walk to where you want to be, and transport yourself back to your initial location along the road to success.

Have you ever heard of a "big lemon" exercise? It's simple. Close your eyes and imagine a big, juicy and sour lemon. Imagine how you wash it, peel it, slice it and finally put it in your mouth. Do you feel your saliva glands immediately start to work? Imagination and visualization trigger some bodily reactions and emotions.

- **Do It!**

Completing an action involves accountability. Be accountable for your own success. Put an expiration date on your goal and observe quality control by establishing benchmarks. Remain focused on your goal. Last, but certainly not the least, get set and **go for it!**

I always recommend getting an "accountability" buddy. Getting a personal coach would be perfect, but very few people can afford it. The good news is that you can become your own coach. All you need to do is to find a person you look up to as far as certain area of life is concerned. For example, if your goals are centered on financial wellbeing, finding a person that accumulated wealth and remodeling what they did is the best strategy to follow.

It can be someone you know, or just someone you connected to online. Listening to them and following in their footsteps will not be enough. You also need to apply and sometimes even question what they say. Don't be afraid to ask them questions so that you can learn and progress. Tell them about your goals. They will tell you that it's possible and totally doable as they managed to achieve it. Here's the important thing - look for people who actually practice what they preach, not just someone who claims to be a "guru."

For example, if you are searching for financial success, which would you choose as your coach?
1. A person who was born poor and thanks to his/her determination, creativity and mindset, managed to accumulate wealth and is now teaching people the secrets of attracting abundance.
2. Someone who is a certified financial adviser, coach and accountant. They were born wealthy, went to college, got an education and are now teaching people how to get rich, even though they never had to struggle.

I would choose person number 1 because I can relate to them more. It's up to you which you decide to choose. Nothing is black or white. You can meet a person who is a combination of both (For example, they were born lower middle class, accumulated wealth, and they also have certified education, or someone who was born rich, but were cut off buy their parents so that they could learn how to achieve things themselves.).

Use your intuition. I am not telling you what to do.

The key is to find someone who is an expert in a field you wish to master and they have verifiable results they achieved themselves.

Programs and seminars are also a great recommendation as you will meet other people, like you, on the same wavelength. You will meet people who want to be successful. You can make many new friends and get new, reliable accountability buddies.

There are a couple things you should know about programs and seminars: be careful not to pick a scam, and secondly, don't overdo it. Here's my opinion - I know lots of people who attend one seminar after another, and purchase plenty of motivational programs and other products, but they never take action. They acquire knowledge but they never get inspired to finally transform their lives. Be careful and apply what you learn.

"To know and not to apply is really not to know"- Jim Rohn.

Chapter 3: NLP for Perfect Relationships

Since NLP tackles how to communicate positively with yourself and others for success, it can forge cooperative and lasting relationships. One of the best ways to harness linguistics for perfect relationships is through rapport. In fact, rapport is one of the four pillars of NLP.

Rapport refers to creating alignment or connection with another person. Rapport is important in fostering cooperative relationships because without rapport, people tend to harbor feelings of being ignored, not being cared about or listened to. The common consequences of the absence or lack of rapport in communication are misunderstanding and resistance. As one builds rapport with other people, feelings of appreciation, familiarity, and understanding are fostered. When these feelings are evoked, most people respond positively.

In other words, it all comes down to working on your intuition and empathy. I used to be really set in my ways and now I understand that those who I was close to found it difficult to put up with me. No matter how simple the conversation was, I always had to be right. I did not know how to listen, but I wanted others to listen to me. It's no wonder that I would struggle in my relationships. I just wanted others to sit quiet and to obey. What a horrible mistake! I would usually get myself into unnecessary arguments with my girlfriends, colleagues, family, my best friends, and even my bosses. Many people would complain about my "character" but I would just stick to my belief that I am always right and it's their fault.

The truth is it's not always someone else's fault. It may also be your fault. Sometimes we are so deeply stuck with our beliefs that we do whatever it takes, we delude ourselves, and don't want to reach the depth of truth.

Let me illustrate with this story I heard from a friend of mine who is a life coach and psychologist.

There is a patient and a therapist. The reason for the therapy is that the patient believes he is dead. He even sleeps in a coffin. The therapist tries everything he can to make the patient realize that he is alive. He tells him that he can talk, walk, eat and sleep and wake up. He is alive.

Yet the patient does not want to believe in it. Finally, the therapist asks him, "Do dead people bleed?"
The patient answers, "No, they don't. Of course they don't. This is not possible."
 The therapist then decides to take a needle to slightly scratch

the patient's finger. And so he does. As a result, the patient's finger starts bleeding. The therapist asks him, "So, what do you think now? You see, you are not dead, because you are bleeding. You are alive."

Guess what the patient says?
"Oh, my God! Dead people do bleed sometimes!."

The patient can be compared to a person who is so set in his or her ways that they are willing to live in delusion (rather than shift their mindset). This is because the truth can be painful and they don't want to recognize it. They have built their own foundation. They don't want to destroy it.

Now, what is your foundation and how does it work for you?

Many of my relationships were like this and now I laugh at myself. I have made lots of mistakes, but I have also learned from them. Still, if you can do it right straight from the beginning, I suggest you do it RIGHT and work with NLP to take your relationships to a whole new level. I hurt so many people that will never talk to me again no matter how hard I try now. This is the price I had to pay for this lesson.

Matching and Mirroring

In NLP, the common rapport-building strategies are matching

and mirroring. These techniques involve adopting the same point of view, position or tone as the other person, as you interact with him/her. Search for clues that will help you ascertain what a person you want to create rapport with is thinking. Once you gain some hints or insight about what he/she might be thinking about an issue of interest, verify the accuracy of such information and endeavor to respond positively.

I am not talking about "not being yourself" or "killing your personality." I am not telling you to act in the same manner as those around you only to gain their approval. We are going deeper here. It's about understanding why others feel and act the way they do.

Matching and mirroring may also be practiced the other way around. You can model behavior that will reflect the state or idea you want others to feel about you. To illustrate, if you want to gain the confidence of your superior and explain that you are capable of handling the PR team bound for Japan, and you see a poster with Nihongo characters pinned on the mini corkboard in his office, you can either:

- Research the English translation of the poster message and attempt to voice out to him in a casual way that you agree with the premise of his Japanese quote;

- Learn the actual Japanese quote in Nihongo, research similar quotes in Japanese including proper accent, and show that you learn the foreign language well and quickly.

The effect of your matching and mirroring from the first technique will build rapport with him by showing you are in agreement about the Japanese quote.

You can gain his confidence that you can act as team lead because your perspectives concur, in other words, you are on the same page. In the second technique, you match and mirror by reflecting the state that you are very interested in learning Japanese and you are a quick learner. You can gain his confidence because a PR team hinges on communication. You have the obvious edge because you impressed him with the Nihongo terms you learned.

This strategy can be really helpful in your professional life, your business and job interviews.

Create Warm Rapport Now: Important Hints
Building rapport is not just about the message or the content of the message. Rapport is also influenced by:

- Voice: Emulate the vocal qualities of the other person's manner of speaking;

- Breathing: Synchronize your rate of breathing with the person you intend to create rapport with;

- Movement and energy levels: A person who moves fast and full of energy responds positively to another person with about the same pace of movement of energy level. If the other person seems somewhat lethargic, build rapport by slowing down your pace to his or her level;

- Body language: Be careful about mirroring gestures and facial expressions because you might be mistaken for mimicking the other person and it might be misconstrued for negative intent. Wait a few seconds before mirroring body language.

Recognizing and Eliminating Negative and Disempowering Beliefs about Relationships

PROFESSIONAL RELATIONSHIPS
"I will never get a raise or a better job offer because I don't have enough contacts. Success is only achieved if you know people who can help you and recommend your profile to potential employers."

If this is your belief, ask yourself WHY this is what you believe in. Was it because of your experiences? Did someone from your family tell you this when you were a kid? Did someone tell you that success is a lottery? First, analyze it carefully and try to find the WHY. Maybe those around you who have well-paid jobs got them thanks to their acquaintances. So what? It's up to you to decide what to focus on. There are many successful people who are from humble backgrounds and yet they managed to get a pay raise or their dream job! Then, reframe it with this example:

"I am a talented and creative human being. I learn new skills everyday and there are plenty of companies who will welcome me with open arms. I depend on myself and my own actions. I create my professional path."

Again, this is only an example. I suggest you do it yourself to personalize it with your own positive language.

Aside from the linguistic side, try to surround yourself with people who are achievers and people who managed to build up their professional career themselves with their own work. Their examples and their actions will also help you change your mind set about professional success.

"I am a slow learner and I don't have time to learn new things. This is why I can't get a better job."

Again, ask yourself why you think that way? Is it because of the fact that schooling system usually does not recognize individual efforts and talents and only wants kids to fill in and abide by certain standards? Who told you are a slow learner? Your teacher? Your parents? Do you know what Albert Einstein was told when he was in school? He was actually called a "slow learner." Did this stop him from achieving success and contributing to the world?

Perhaps you are not a slow learner. Perhaps you just don't do much to learn or you don't know HOW to learn.

I know many people who were struggling in school, yet they managed to achieve a lot thanks to self-education. Also, if you say, "I don't have time," it sounds as if you were trying to justify the fact that you are a slow learner, which is not true anyway.

In order to reframe it, you should say:
"I am committed to self-education. I find time to improve myself and get new skills regularly".

"I never do well during job interviews because I get really nervous. I forget what to say and I always tremble. I don't want to look like an idiot. Another job interview? No, thank you!"

Well, actually, the more you say it, the more you interact with your subconscious mind and the more nervous you will become as a result. If you believe that you will be nervous then it will always stay that way. For example, I used to go red all the time. It was really embarrassing. Very often, I would blush just at the mere thought that I may go red and that people would laugh at me. Thanks to NLP, I was able to realize WHY this was happening. I recalled an event from my childhood when I was in school and other students would laugh at me calling me a "beetroot." This is why I was really obsessed about going or rather not going red, because I did not want to be in the center of attention. And, of course, as a result I would usually go red. It was a vicious circle.

I decided to create my own anchor. I went back to my childhood when I was on a vacation with my grandparents, feeling taken care of and secure. I would press my left elbow (You may create whatever physical representation you wish. You could touch your neck, knee, or something else. It's up to you.) when thinking about it. It was my anchor. Then, I visualized the most stressful public speaking event I could expose myself to. I went through all the steps in my mind, feeling peace, calmness and security. Pressing my elbow would immediately make me feel relaxed and I would go back to the nice memory I had with my grandparents. I would do this exercise every day and then, I finally got in touch with my local community and decided to speak at some of the local events. The mere act of practicing public speaking would make me feel more confident. I never blushed again. I just focused my attention on connecting to my listeners.

Again, you should step back and think of the WHY. Who or what caused it?

The way you can reframe it is:

"I feel confident as there are plenty of natural solutions and relaxation techniques. I am committed to mastering them. I will do well during my job interview and I will learn a lot from this experience. Success is mine."

PERSONAL

My friend, Jane, had what is often called "Really bad luck with boyfriends."

She would always end up in negative relationships and very often, her boyfriends would cheat on her and even abuse her emotionally and physically. Her belief was:

"All men are dishonest and unfaithful. I will never find my true love. Love does not exist in the real world. It only exists in the movies, not in real life!"

No wonder she would always end up with yet another "bad boy"! Needless to say, she would blame the circumstances.

Most people would say that Jane had bad luck with boyfriends, just like some people have "bad luck" with businesses, work and finances. I decided to talk to her. I mean, we had been friends for many years, we grew up together and so Jane was like a sister to me. I asked her what, in her opinion, was the problem. She said: "Well, I have bad luck. Maybe it's my karma? I always fall in love with the wrong guy and then I suffer. I think I don't deserve to be in a healthy and nurturing relationship. Those men pick me up for a reason."

As you can imagine, it was quite a task to reprogram her. I first told her that it was her own fault. That she was picking the wrong guys as she believed that she did not deserve anyone better. It turned out that this belief was ingrained in her when she was a kid. Her dad would also cheat on her mom and eventually abandoned them for another woman. Hence, Jane, as a little girl, thought that it was her fault. There is always more than just one issue to be exposed.

At first, we worked on her self-talk and we made it positive. Then, we worked on her goals, using the SMART philosophy. It was difficult at first, as she still needed more time to change her way of thinking.

I would tell her, "Hey Jane, imagine that there are 5 good-looking blokes in front of your house. They all have the qualities of your perfect guy. They are waiting for you and you can just go and pick and choose one." Again, at first, she would not believe it. I would tell her: "How about if there were 20 good looking blokes...or 200? Or 200,000? Or even more than that? You can pick and choose!"

She finally understood that she is in control. She first involved herself in a few relationships that ended rather fast, but it was because she ended them, not the other way around. Finally, she met her soul mate when volunteering for her local community. They are now engaged. Now they are one of the most loving couples I have ever seen. Jane wants to use her experience to help women who are physically and emotionally abused. She wants to make them realize that not all men are bastards (excuse my language please).

FINAL EXERCISE
Control your mind. Watch it and observe it. Analyze it. You can't just change your life without realizing the truth about yourself first.
There are plenty of factors that made you who you are, some of them influenced you in a positive way, and some of them in a negative way. Brainstorm and analyze:
-past events
-traumas
-illnesses

-friends and family and what you were told by them

-your country and your culture

I have another story for you. Let's keep it brief. My friend, Linda, was a very independent and hard-working woman and she was really into her professional life. While on a vacation in Italy, she fell in love with a charming Italian guy. She decided to leave her native England and move to sunny Italy. Sounds awesome, right? Unfortunately, after a few years of living in beautiful Italy, she began to feel depressed. Even though she learned perfect Italian and she loved her husband, she did not get on well with his family and friends. According to her, the Italian culture is a bit "machista" which means that nobody respected her professional life and her independence. She wanted to fit in, so she quit her job and became a housewife. Now, I do believe that there is nothing wrong with becoming a housewife, but it was not for Linda. She felt stuck and unfulfilled. She decided to go back to work, but her husband was not supportive at all. She would obey him again, feeling torn between the culture she grew up in (an independent English women) and the small Italian town's mentality. She was trying to fit in, and it was actually against her rules. Her depression was probably because of the inner conflict that the cultural clashes brought on her.

Thanks to NLP, she understood the limiting beliefs that a new culture ingrained in her. Following my advice, she took pride in her English roots and decided to have her say. She told her husband that she wanted to move to a bigger city, and get back to work as an English teacher. Her husband would not understand her. He would tell her that he would pay for everything and so she need not to work. This is what many people in his village were doing. Linda, however, reprogrammed herself back to the "original" Linda and moved to Rome by herself. Her husband did not follow her as he preferred to stay with his mother. Linda asked for a divorce as she realized that the relationship she had would not respect her personal or cultural beliefs. She now lives and works in Rome and met a new guy who respects her values. Thanks to NLP she was able to understand the way she was negatively conditioning herself just to "fit in." Also, many friends would say that during that time that Linda was not Linda, but some other girl. She began acting, talking and thinking as her ex husband's family and friends.

This is only an example. I traveled to Italy many times, and I mean no offense to Italians. Not all Italian men are machistas and not all Italian women quit work as soon as they get married.

Chapter 4 NLP for Improved Health and Vitality?

According to motivational coach and speaker, Jenny Camilo, "Healing begins first in your mind." (Camilo[1]) Likewise, international educator and seminar leader Deb Shapiro affirms that your body manifests what is in your mind. (Shapiro[2]) These are just a couple of parallelisms that your mind affects your body and your health. This suggests that you can apply NLP strategies to enhance your motivation in caring for your health and improve your vitality. This strategy can be combined with all kinds of diets and treatments (standard, preventative, natural or alternative) and is 100% safe.

NLP Strategies Pertaining to Selected Health Issues

- Freedom from phobias and release of painful memories

People cannot just deal with a phobia or extreme fear of anything that causes anxiety on the afflicted individual by simply showing the body who's the boss. To be free from phobia is to successfully attempt to change the feeling associated with the thought that causes the fear. NLP strategies can help handle phobias and painful memories. The two most common strategies are association and dissociation.

Association is experiencing or viewing the world through a person's own body. Meanwhile, dissociation is experiencing or seeing the world outside of your own body, or in other words as observer. As a tool, NLP helps people to dissociate from a bad or painful memory by associating the experience with neutral feelings. You finally realize that there is no place for fear. You look at your situation from a different perceptive. As a result, your perception of a fearful situation can be changed. People use it to successfully overcome all kinds of fears and phobias (for example: fear of public speaking , or a fear of water).

Sources:
1 Camilo, J. (2013). *Secrets of healing*. Bloomington, IN: Balboa Press.

2 Shapiro, D. (2008). *Your body speaks your mind*. Sydney: Read How You Want

To illustrate, if your fear has something to do with an experience about fire, you actually get released from your phobia by reliving the experience not as the one being in a fire situation, but an interested observer like watching a picture or a video of a fire. You model behavior that reacts to the video simply as a spectator that is not directly entangled with the complications of the incident. Simply put, through NLP you dissociate yourself from the sorrow of the ordeal.

- Relieving anxiety and stress

Stress is a common challenge among a lot of people. Stress affects not just how you perform tasks, but your quality of life and your health. However, relieving anxiety and stress is more than just thinking calm and peaceful thoughts. Fortunately, NLP has an effective arsenal of tools to enhance your life and vitality.

One way by which NLP addresses stress and anxiety issues is by "mapping across." This tool allows a person to transfer an identity or skill from one situation into another. It facilitates taking resources from one state to another.

To illustrate there is a superb salesperson, Jade, who has been referred to as someone who can convince the stingiest prospect to buy an item for sale. However, when she goes home, she always has conflicts with her husband because they can't seem to agree on anything. With mapping across, she is guided to identify her strong people skills such as her gift of glib and power of persuasion in the workplace and use it to enhance her relationship with her husband.

In mapping out, instead of her identity as a wife, Jade takes on her identity as an effective salesperson. To be successful at mapping out, her husband is then regarded as a client and the issue they have to agree on is transformed to an item for sale. Confident that she can always make a sale, Jade then transfers her skills in the workplace to family life to establish rapport and sell the idea to her husband.

To make it simple, I call it "tags" or "labeling oneself." You can label yourself as a peaceful and stress-free person and practice this skill in the environments that don't make you feel stressed. Record the image and the feeling of relaxation using all your senses. You will feel confident knowing that you know how to relax. Now, all you need to do is to remember to recall this feeling in places and situations that would make you feel stressed out, nervous or anxious.

Look at the situation as if you were watching it from outside. You are an observer. Now you know that you can shift your mindset and your perception. You can create your new, stress-free reality.

- Kicking undesirable behavior

It takes more than willpower to do away with an unwanted behavior. Many of the undesirable ones are vital to your health and success and you need NLP to stop such unhealthy habits. For example, the practice of over-eating. Anne's husband loves her so much but lately, she always engages in heated discussions with him because he is worried about her weight. Anne was so frustrated because she had tried several times to eat healthier, but she ends up on a food binge.

The process of visualization has always worked wonders. Anne tried NLP via visualization and created a visual. Here is the image she created:

She is eating a small portion of healthy foods: fruits, vegetables, tuna, and very little rice. She is eating very slowly, takes a couple of hours to rest, and then she walks casually on the sand in a skimpy bikini. All the guys can't help but admire her great figure.

She then approaches her husband and the two of them walk while holding hands on the shore. Details play an important role here. They talk about the results of her general check-up and she is in perfect health. They make the sweetest embrace that fades in a silhouette.

Anne opens her eyes feeling very good about her visual. Whenever she sees food and feels the urge to eat a lot, she would close her eyes and relive the visual. After a year, she was able to kick her overeating habit. Now, her visual is a reality. Aside from the pleasure of looking sexy and skinny, she also associated health to it. The feeling of wellness, health, vitality and excellent check-up results makes her happier. After all, she did not want to end up with serious health issues that overeating could lead her to. Putting on weight is only the tip of the iceberg.

Stay Healthy!
NLP is a positive approach to life and success. Transform your life and maintain a healthy life. Do it and enjoy!

Possible limiting beliefs

"I will never lose weight."

"Losing weight is hard."

"Health is difficult."

"Eating healthy is really expensive and extremely time-consuming."

"I am not good at sports. My parents were never interested in sports."

"All my friends and family eat unhealthy and it would be impossible for me to start a new diet."

"I don't have enough will power to quit smoking/eat healthy/go to the gym."

Needless to say, these are all limiting beliefs that may stop you from achieving success. Chances are that those who give in to their own disempowering thoughts will not even prepare a plan to take action.

It is also important to realize WHY you are preventing yourself from health success. Do you remember my own weight loss story? Remember, there is always at least one person in the world who can be your role model. There is always someone who managed to achieve what you are now asking for.

Millions of people, who embarked on a health and wellness journey, love it so much, that they don't want to get back to where they were before. Health is their lifestyle. I am one of them. Imagine that you are in an abusive and unhappy relationship. You finally leave your partner and you find your soul mate. You start an amazing relationship and finally get married. Would you like to go back to your ex- partner? The same thing applies to a healthy lifestyle, diets and physical activity. This is why I don't see any reason why you can't start eating healthy and going to the gym NOW. Use NLP to guide you on your path to healthfulness. Health is pleasure, right?

The truth is that there are so many things that we want as kids, and as kids, we imagine that it is going to be easy. The more we grow, the more bitter we become, and this is very often negative social programming. Beliefs such as, "you can't have it all," or, "as you get old, you will feel tired, and there is nothing you can do about it" (where there actually is, just take care of your body and mind), "you are asking for too much", "you must be like other people," are all limiting beliefs that you should strive to eradicate from your life.

Do they sound familiar to you, my dear reader?

Exercise
Analyze your situation and your health, fitness and wellness goals. First, be honest with yourself and write down all of your beliefs. They may be disempowering just like the examples

above.

Now, go through the list and rewrite them, using the tools we have discussed earlier. Use strong and positive language that expresses confidence. Read your new beliefs aloud. Keep the list in your wallet, in your office or even laminated in your bathroom. You can also stick it on your fridge. Use visual representation too. Find your health role models. Get inspired by their lifestyle.

Formulate your goals using the SMART strategy. Feel the victory and don't forget to take action.

Finally, create your own healthy lifestyle. You will have NLP to thank when you start seeing results!

Chapter 5 NLP to Attract Money

It's no joke; some people can't really get it going with money no matter how hard they work for it. You have to believe that it is not always what you do and how you do it. It first has to come from how you think. Yes, what you think deep within the recesses of your subconscious matters with respect to money. With NLP strategies, you can program your subconscious to help with your money goals.

As far as negative money and wealth beliefs are concerned, I can definitely relate to them. They used to be a part of my lifestyle and my general perception of the world. It's no wonder I was always working extremely hard, yet ended up being frustrated and very often in debt. It took me many years to understand that the problem was not the fact that I was not born in a rich or influential family, but it was my own disempowering view on money, wealth, rich people, and financial wellness. We will talk more about it at the end of this chapter.

Guided Imagery to Turn Yourself into a Money Machine: The 10 Steps to Attract Money the NLP Way

Step 1: Assess your money mentality

For a clear view, list your beliefs about money in 2 columns: positive and negative. Those beliefs or ideas may be passed on to you by other people or you may have read them in books, magazines, etc.

Step 2: Use guided imagery to discard your negative thoughts about money by thinking of the opposite or something that might prove that negative thought wrong.

To illustrate, if your father gave you the idea that no matter how hard you work, you won't have enough money, throw that idea away. Create a visual of you at present with your financial state; say you have a thousand dollars in your account. Picture that and see yourself working hard to turn it to millions. You see your balance in the bank account increasing, you keep working hard and you enjoy what you do.

You buy a nice car. You smell the scent of your triumph. You enjoy the vivid color - it's your favorite color and model. Drive it and feel how happy you are driving it and going places. Continue the image with all the nice things happening in your life because you are making money.

Step 3: Return to reality and talk to yourself positively to attract money.

*This was discussed in Chapter 2. Revisit it. You will do a lot of self talk in NLP.

Step 4: As you talk to your subconscious, telling yourself that you choose to attract money and make lots of it, partner your reinforcing language with the corresponding actions.

If you make money by selling, make your move and do selling in the best and most positive way. It may be challenging, but always go back to the feeling you imagined - where you feel really good working to make money. Always get back to that powerful imagery of having lots of money every time you feel tired, helpless or like losing hope. Never forget that image.

Step 5: Get inspiration from a role model.

Your role model is someone you admire because he or she excels at making money. Motivate yourself and think of your role model. He or she didn't give up, and neither will you.

Step 6: Do not put a limit in your thoughts about how much money you can make.

Is there any reason why you limit yourself when it comes to money? What's the point of thinking that you can make only $X a month? Why not add a few more '000' to it?

Step 7: Repeat the same process of discarding negative money beliefs until all that you have in mind is a positive belief system about money.

It's not enough to just think these thoughts. You need to feel them with your body, spirit, and mind. Positivity will lead you to follow through with your actions. These actions will assist you in acquiring what you really want.

Step 8: Reinforce positive thoughts and your belief system with adequate work. Attend professional development opportunities and continue learning personal skills that will assist you in your life's journey.

Step 9: Never ignore your spiritual well-being.

At the end of the day, no matter how much money you rake in, you want to be happy and content. You have great thoughts and an equally great set of personal and professional skills. Make sure you enrich your soul with unending prayers, praises, and thanks to Divine Providence.

Step 10: Go ahead and attract money yourself.

You will be amazed at how easy it is to attract money and keep it coming. It all comes down to changing your mindset. You may be subconsciously stopping yourself from financial success. Just remember, if you intently think that you can make money, you can do it; but never forget to learn lifelong skills and aim for continuous professional development. **All systems must be involved - mind, body, and soul!**

Finally, let's brainstorm again. Below are some of my old money beliefs versus my new beliefs. It's totally up to you to change the way you believe to suit your needs and wants. I am not telling you what to do. This exercise is not about being right or wrong.

However, if you want to be financially successful, I encourage you to reflect back on your own beliefs. Analyze them. Your mind, the way you speak with others and even talk to yourself can be your biggest problem.

I have a friend who is just starting to develop his own software and applications. He really loves what he does, technology is his passion. He is extremely talented and I know that his talent can contribute to the world. Yesterday, we caught up for a drink, and I told him, "I am sure that you will be soon making $100, 000 a month or more!" Now my friend, Tom, is not even making that amount of money a year. In fact, he has always been struggling with debt.

His reaction was, "I don't even need that much money. It would feel bad to have that much. I am not used to having lots of money. I think it's not for me."

What do you think? He probably thought that money was evil. Yet, he worked so hard (all his life) for it, only to be struggling financially. His new business was supposed to help him gain financial freedom and there he was again sabotaging himself with his own thoughts.

I am in the process of helping him reprogram himself with NLP. Here is what I told him:
-If you don't need that much money that's totally fine. You can still carry on your minimalist lifestyle. However, with that amount of money, you will be able to contribute to society. Think about it! You can use it to help other people. You could even start your own company and create jobs. You could use your money to run a charity. You could help those who are struggling with income get education. Your parents are still paying their mortgage and they have no savings. You could help them too. You could buy an apartment for your sister, and pay for her education so she could leave her mind-numbing job and do what she loves (she wants to become a school teacher).
-Contribution - with your skills and ideas, you can create products and services that help people. There is nothing wrong with making money from a good service or product. You are not stealing from anybody.

-Responsibility - again I told him to imagine how his products will become really popular and how he will begin getting more and more money. I told him to think of at least 10 ways to use his income to help other people. Then I told him - you see? If you say that you don't deserve to be making $100,000 a month, those people out there, won't be able to receive your help.

-Positive Self-Talk - Finally, Tom was able to redefine his new mission. He sounded confident and spoke with security and passion for developing new products and making money.

We changed his thinking to say, "I am passionate about creating software and application products that help other people. Next year, I will be easily making $100,000 a month. I will use my income to help those who want to study, yet struggle financially. I will also start my own non-profit organization. My money can help me, my family and other people. I deserve to be making tons of money. Money is freedom and it can help me make a difference in the world. I will eventually become a millionaire, who will be using his abundance to serve others. I will prove to the world that money is help, freedom and happiness and that rich people are good people!"

You see? He has totally changed his associations. Now he no longer sees money as something bad, but quite the contrary!

His new mission gave him more motivation to work and develop his first product.

You will hear about this guy soon.

EXERCISE

Ask yourself: what are my money making beliefs? Do they make it easier or harder for me to attract abundance? How can I reprogram myself?

OLD: It's impossible to get rich if you were born poor.
NEW: You can get rich even if you were born poor. Many people have. You just need the right strategy and mindset.

OLD: Rich people are not spiritual and too materialistic.
NEW: Spirituality does not depend on being rich or poor. There are also poor people who get caught in a daily struggle, and they don't have time to develop their spirituality. If I create more abundance and financial freedom for myself, I will have more time to learn all about spirituality. This is why money can be helpful.

OLD: One needs to be really lucky to get rich.
NEW: In order to get rich, one needs to work smart. It all comes down to having the right strategy and mindset. I can change my mindset and learn from those who attracted

abundance and financial freedom. This is why I can also become rich. I can create it for myself.

OLD: *In order to get rich, I will need to work a lot and this is not healthy.*

NEW: I can get rich and still keep healthy. It's easy to learn all about time management and productivity. The world is abundant in books, programs, and other resources. I can learn how to manage my time and become more productive. I will have plenty of time to work smart on my businesses and projects as well as to eat healthy and exercise.

OLD: *The problem with making tons of money is that I may lose it and get depressed as a result.*

NEW: People get depressed when they don't grow and create. In order to be happy, you GOTTA BE CREATING.

Making money is not only about the final result. It is also about enjoying the process of getting new financial skills. Having those skills will always allow me to make more money, no matter what. Even if I lose my money, I will have skills to make it back again. Failure forms part of success!

OLD: *I need the right opportunity to make money. Still waiting!*

NEW: I can create my own opportunity NOW. Nobody else is going to create it for me. The key to happiness and abundance lies in creating. The 21 century is abundant and the concept of an online businesses is the best opportunity ever.

OLD: If I want to make more money, I will have to give up doing things I love.
NEW: I can make money doing what I love. My work is my passion.

OLD: I will feel bad making more money than my parents.
NEW: I want to help my parents. When I get rich, they will feel proud of me. I will be able to provide for them and the rest of my family.

OLD: It's really difficult to make lots of money.
NEW: Making money is easy if you pick up the right path and enjoy the process that will also transform your mentality. Thousands of people make money online doing what they love. People make money with companies such as Amazon, eBay and ClickBank. If they can do it, I can do it too. I am grateful for the internet and technology and the thousands of business models it provides.

OLD: It takes years to save up money in order to invest it and make more. I don't think I can make it.
NEW: I am so grateful I live in the 21st century with so many opportunities that the internet is creating. Thanks to the

internet, I can start an online business and there will be a smaller investment requirement. It's possible to make something out of nothing. I can create multiple streams of steady income with zero or almost no investment.

OLD: *It's hard to be making money these days; the economy is to blame. Those who are rich have rich parents or married someone rich.*
NEW: Those who are good money makers can make money even during difficult times of war and recession. Everyone can master the skill of making money. It all comes down to thinking outside the box.

OLD: *In order to be financially free, I will need a steady job and then, hopefully, get promoted.*
NEW: In order to be financially free, I need to learn how to take the risk of creating my own business that offers limitless possibilities.

OLD: *As long as I am healthy and in a loving relationship, I am OK with being poor.*
NEW: I choose to improve all areas of my life. I deserve to be healthy, loved and rich. I deserve to have it all. I want to use all my human potential and inspire others through my abundant lifestyle.

Conclusion: Program Your Way for Success!

Thank you again for taking interest in this book!

I hope that I was able to help you to have a better perspective of how to find success by tapping the unique strategies and tools of Neuro-Linguistic Programming (NLP). With NLP, success is within your reach. With it, you can harness the magnificent power of your mind to program yourself for success. Remember that your mind is more powerful than any computer that man will ever be able to create. This is because you were created by a Supreme Being- God. Who can be more powerful than God? No manmade central processing unit (CPU) can outthink your mind.

With NLP, you can tap the power of your mind to achieve a goal, kick a bad habit, release a phobia, get rid of painful memories, attract money, enjoy financial freedom, stay healthy, get healed of a disease, and be the person you've always wanted to be - a success

To your success,
James

Free eBook & Newsletter- Exclusive Information & Inner Circle Updates

Are you interested in personal development and related topics?

Join *our Holistic Wellness Books Newsletter* & start receiving the most revolutionary tips to help you on your journey.

You will be the first one to find out about our latest releases (eBooks, books, audiobooks and courses) and receive amazing discounts and bonuses!

As a welcome gift, you will receive a **free copy** of our bestselling eBook: *"Affirmations"*:

www.bitly.com/affirmationsfree

23405020R00072

Printed in Poland
by Amazon Fulfillment
Poland Sp. z o.o., Wrocław